Owners

C000111839

BDO Stoy Hayward specialises in helping businesses, whether start-ups or multinationals, to grow. By working directly with fast-track organisations – and the entrepreneurs behind them – we've developed a robust understanding of the factors that govern business growth. BDO Stoy Hayward is a member of the BDO International network, the world's fifth largest accountancy organisation, with representation in more than ninety countries.

Rupert Merson is a partner in BDO Stoy Hayward, where he specialises in helping growing businesses with their people and organisational development problems. Rupert took first-class honours and a university prize in English from Oxford University. He is a chartered accountant and a Fellow of the Chartered Institute of Personnel and Development. He teaches a course on the management of the growing business at London Business School and writes frequently in the national press. He lives in south London with his wife and four children. He's a musician on the side.

Owners

A BDO Stoy Hayward Guide for
Growing Businesses

Rupert Merson

P

PROFILE BOOKS

First published in Great Britain in 2004 by
PROFILE BOOKS LTD
58A Hatton Garden
London EC1N 8LX
www.profilebooks.co.uk

Copyright © BDO Stoy Hayward LLP 2004
8 Baker Street
London W1U 3LL
www.bdo.co.uk

A CIP catalogue record for this book is available from the British Library.

ISBN 1 86197 682 8

Typeset in Galliard by MacGuru Ltd
info@macguru.org.uk

Printed in Great Britain by
Bookmarque, Croydon, Surrey

While care has been taken to ensure the accuracy of the contents of this book,
it is intended to provide general guidance only and does not constitute
professional advice.

Contents

1

Introduction

THIS IS THE fourth in a series of books on the key roles in the owner-managed business with ambitions to grow. The first three in the series focused on active management or director roles – the finance director, the managing director and the non-executive director. The role of the owner is different from these, but at the same time includes elements of them all.

Owning a business is a very different activity from running a business. The fact that owner-managers have to master both owning and managing doesn't make the activities one and the same. Indeed, one of the reasons why the role of owner-manager is so difficult is that the two activities that are thrown together as owner-and-manager get in each other's way. An owner-manager struggling to sort out his own agenda and priorities is in a weak position compared to someone determined to just be an owner – or indeed just a manager. The fact that business financiers are often happy to be just owners (and then only nominally) helps explain why owner-managers and financiers rarely see eye to eye once the signing ceremony is over. Unlike an owner-manager, a financier has only one thing on his mind.

'If the owner is seriously ambitious for growth he will have to fit his own agenda to the business's – and not the other way round.'

Entrepreneurs often go into business driven by a determination to do their own thing – but this is not the same thing as a determination to own a business. A business-ownership mentality is something that develops. An entrepreneur will turn into a business owner once the business starts to develop a life of its own. Rather than controlling the business directly, the business will be run by managers to whom the owner will be struggling to delegate responsibility and authority. The business will have a culture and a set of values that may well echo and reflect the owner's own personality – but will never-theless now be separately identifiable from her. The owner may wake up in a cold sweat some nights and convince herself that if a job needs doing properly in her business it had best be done by herself – but if she's wise, by the morning she will have remembered the importance of (and not just the diffi-culties inherent in) delegation. She will pay herself a dividend as an owner, rather than the salary or bonus that might be paid to her when she is wearing her manager's hat (although her tax accountant might encourage her to confuse the two). Other than that, her reward as owner will be the satisfaction derived from seeing the business grow in value, and the slug of cash she receives once the business is eventually sold – if that is the route she chooses to follow.

Compared to a manager, an owner will tend to have a longer-term view – longer even than a lifetime. It's ownership that passes down the generations in a family business, for example, not management (something that even family busi-nesses are inclined to forget, as Grandpa insists on interfering in the day-to-day management of the business he founded, long after he's left). The owner will see the relationship between her own agenda and the agenda of her business evolve as the business develops. At the outset the business's agenda will be her agenda; but as the business develops a life and agenda of its own, a tension between the two will develop. If the owner is seriously ambitious for growth she will have to fit her own agenda to the business's – and not the other way round. Many owners are not prepared for the nec-essary sacrifices, and take the foot off the pedal to spend more time on the beach, enjoying the fruit of their labours. And although a 'lifestyle' business such as this might be satisfying for the owner, it is a compromise for the business itself. If the business gets through this stage, the agenda of the owner will increasingly become an irrelevance – and this too can be a difficult experience.

This book discusses these difficulties, and many more complications that threaten the life of the business owner. As with other titles in this series, it benefits from the experience of many individuals who have faced up to these difficulties in their own experience of owner-management. Hopefully their lessons can become yours.

- Owning a business is different from running one. Some people confuse the two
- The business will develop a different, often conflicting, agenda from that of the owner

2

Types of ownership

OWNERSHIP COMES IN many guises. In this chapter I discuss some of the most common manifestations of ownership that those involved in growing, entrepreneurial businesses are likely to come across.

Ownership and finance

At the outset it's worth drawing a distinction between ownership and finance. Of course, the owners of a business are a fundamental source of finance for the business. When the buck stops it won't stop with the bank. But because financiers play with all sorts of 'instruments' when structuring their offers, and many of these instruments are technically forms of ownership, it is only too easy to assume that ownership is merely a financing mechanism – and ownership is much more complicated than that. Owner-managers and entrepreneurs normally see themselves as owners rather than financiers. Financiers might talk of being their clients' 'partners', but the famously uncomfortable relationship between financiers and entrepreneurs gives the lie to this particular notion of partnership and the sharing in ownership it implies.

'A new business is often impossible to identify separately from its founding owner.'

Labels such as 'debt finance' and 'equity finance' don't help, suggesting as they do some sort of choice between the two when seeking to finance the business. Some forms of finance are difficult to categorise as either debt or equity. The fact that the technical title ends in '...share' or '...loan stock' may indicate the legal form, but not the practical reality of the instrument. In general terms, if it's difficult to tell, then it's probably debt in disguise, and the supplier will behave more like a creditor than an owner – someone more interested in their investment than in their business. An entrepreneur needs to know whether he's looking at a piece of debt masquerading as equity, and negotiating with a potential shareholder who's going to behave just like a bank manager when the ink is dry on the investment documentation.

By and large if your risk profile is low enough, and your security is good enough, financiers will be desperate to lend you money – usually, of course, when you don't need it. In all other circumstances you will have to look either to the business for self-generated funds or to the owners; and if the current owners don't have enough then the business may need new owners – or some additional owners. In these circumstances the latter should be assessed for their ownership credentials as much as, or more than, if they were potential sources of finance.

What are the real characteristics of ownership? Ownership is best understood as the ultimate source of capital for the business, and capital is best understood not just in financial terms. Of course owners are the people who have to write the first cheques – or persuade others to write the cheques. But a good definition of 'capital' would include fundamentals about what the business is for and what it is trying to achieve. As has been observed elsewhere in this series of books, this starts with the personality of the founder, but as the business develops it will turn into constructs that will be given names such as 'brand', 'values' and 'culture'. These constructs will be managed by the directors and staff employed by the business, but in private business they will be rooted in and dependent on the owners – certainly the founder-owners if they are still holding equity.

This is very different from the experience of share ownership in publicly quoted companies. For most shareholders in quoted companies, whether institutional or private, the motivation is financial and the role is one of *investor* rather than *owner*. There are exceptions of course. In stark contrast to the pension fund manager reviewing his fund's performance is the die-hard football fan, who does not buy shares in his beloved club for financial reasons – at least, I hope he doesn't. And it's a rare pension fund manager who frames the share certificates of the companies in his fund and hangs them on the wall festooned with scarves, signed photographs and other company memorabilia.

Of course, the football fan isn't a model for the owner of most private businesses. But there are elements of the football club shareholder mentality that are shared with the owner-manager of a private business – the identification with the business, the commitment, the passion, the tension between wishing to get involved and the need to delegate authority. These are as much at the heart of ownership as the provision of financial resources and commercial acuity.

Unincorporated businesses – sole traders and partnerships

The form of ownership will more often than not change as the business grows.

Most businesses will start as unincorporated entities, indeed as entities without any specific legal form at all. A new business is often impossible to identify separately from its founding owner. It will operate – if it operates at all – from the founder's bedroom. Its bank account will be the founder's bank account.

As far as the relationship between the business and the owner goes, and the legal form of the business is concerned, many small businesses scarcely get much more sophisticated. Certainly many – even once they have an existence recognisably separate from their founders – will stay as unincorporated businesses, businesses that haven't chosen to incorporate themselves as limited liability companies. Most of these are 'sole traders', businesses that in effect are vehicles for

> **'I had the title,** but I wasn't the CEO because I wasn't the bloke who founded the firm. And he was seen around the business every day.'

one individual to deliver his services, and they share the commercial and financial strengths and weaknesses of the individual – even after the individual has recruited a secretary and a few assistants. Such a 'sole trader' is deemed to be 'self-employed' – though his assistants are likely to be deemed to be 'employed'. As an unincorporated entity, the business will offer no protection to the owner from the outside world. A sole trader in an unincorporated business has unlimited liability for his actions. If a deal goes bad, creditors may go after the owner's personal assets as well as the business's. Financiers will also find it difficult to see any separation between the business and the individual when deciding whether to lend money, and will be lending money to the individual rather than the business. A bank will almost definitely want the owner to sign a personal guarantee, and though it may be possible to haggle over some of the terms (e.g. when the guarantee will be reviewed), it is highly unlikely that the borrower will be able to negotiate it away altogether. On the plus side, businesses like this are not subject to any specific regulation, and are under no pressure to file financial statements.

Partnerships are what happen when more than one sole trader gets together, and they all want to be principals in the business. Partners in a standard partnership are the business's owner-managers. Like sole traders, partners are deemed to be self-employed, which can be useful for tax purposes. Essentially partnerships have all the disadvantages of sole traders, with some inevitable extra complications of scale thrown in. Partners in normal partnerships have unlimited liability. Indeed, they are jointly and severally liable for each others' liabilities – the actions of one partner could conceivably lead to the personal financial ruin of all the partners. Although there are examples of partnerships that have tapped the bond market, it remains relatively difficult for partnerships, even quite substantial partnerships, to raise external finance, and the partnership's finance-raising capacity is essentially the same as the sum of the individual capacities of the partners. The Partnership Act 1890 offers a safety net of legislation to protect from themselves those partnerships that have chosen not to draft partnership agreements to govern their affairs. It sets a base line for hygiene matters such as internal financial reporting timetables – but also rules on some significant issues; for example, that the partnership will automatically

'As an unincorporated entity, the business will offer no protection to the owner from the outside world. A sole trader in an unincorporated business has unlimited liability for his actions.'

dissolve in the event of a partner leaving – which can be quite a nuisance. A partnership wishing to get round this one, and some of the other provisions of the Act, will need a partnership agreement.

But the very fact that partnerships are still governed by a piece of legislation that dates from the century before last (although new proposals are now on the table) suggests that, as a mechanism for sharing ownership, the partnership, for all its drawbacks, has been hugely successful.

The Partnership Act, 1890, establishes certain rights for partners – which will apply if not varied in writing by the partners, ideally using a properly drafted partnership agreement. Some of the following in particular are important to consider:

- The partnership automatically dissolves on the death (or bankruptcy) of any partner
- Any partner can bring the partnership to an end by giving notice to the other partners
- All partners are entitled to share equally in the capital and profits of the business – and are liable to contribute equally to any losses
- All partners have the right to participate in the management of the business
- On dissolution, any losses are to be paid first out of profits, then out of capital, and then by the partners themselves in the proportion in which they are entitled to share profits
- No new partners can join without the agreement of all partners
- Ordinary business can be decided by majority vote
- Partnership accounts must be prepared within ten months of the year end, which will be on 31 March

In part this is a matter of regulation. Many professionals, lawyers and accountants in particular, have been obliged by professional regulations to practise as partnerships regardless of any commercial or personal desire to incorporate. And in recent years there has been plenty of yearning, by accountants in particular, for the haven of incorporation and the limited liability status that this offers its owners. In an increasingly litigious environment, unlimited liability is considered to be very risky. And, once the statutory limit of twenty on the number of partners in a partnership was relaxed for certain types of partnership, many large partnerships have felt less like partnerships and more like incorporated entities anyway. Many of the partners in a 2,000-partner partnership have felt more like employees than partners. If you are beginning to look and feel like an incorporated corporation, why not become one? The 'Limited Liability Partnership' (not to be confused with the 'Limited Partnership') has been invented as a compromise to allow partners in partnerships, whilst retaining some of the benefits of unincorporation (including tax benefits), some of the protection allowed to the owners of limited companies in return for a requirement to file audited financial information. 'LLP' status, governed by the Limited Liability Partnership Act 2000, gives to a partnership an identity separate from the partners – though in many ways this is giving legal recognition to what for some partners has substantially been the case anyway.

But the LLP story is a bit of a red herring, and should not be used to suggest that the partnership model is dead. Far from it. There are good reasons why partnerships work. No business structure fosters a closer identification between the owners and the guts of the business itself. You can think of it as a manifestation of the old 'gentlemen's club' if you wish, but being a partner in a partnership does give a curious sense of belonging, ownership and shared commitment that fancy talk about 'brand' and 'culture' and 'values' sometimes struggles hard to emulate. For years, large limited companies have sought to reduce their layers of middle management and empower a greater number of senior individuals, but partnerships have had no need to – they have been there all the time. Partnerships are also peculiarly well suited to knowledge-based businesses. Despite the knowledge management revolution, knowledge businesses' assets continue to be contained between the ears of the principal individuals in the business. A knowledge business will always be based on the personal relationship between an individual adviser and his client. A partnership allows the individual to take advantage of scale, and the efficiencies to be derived from working in close proximity with someone with complementary skills – but it is still in essence a collection of individuals. For this reason, partnerships – despite a recent yearning to incorporate – have usually found it difficult to establish corporate cultures.

Many partnerships find it difficult to separate their strengths from their weaknesses. Even well-managed partnerships are organisations led by individuals in which it is difficult for any one individual to get the upper hand, or at least for long. With so much competition at the top, partnerships could be considered to be inherently divisive, but they can't survive without consensus. Getting consensus has been likened to trying to herd cats, but a good firm will reach consensus in the end, which will significantly reduce the risk of individual partners doing daft things. A mature partnership structure is therefore not the route for the single owner who wants to carry on calling all the shots. But neither will it lead to shredding skip-loads of documents; only a partnership that has actually turned into a corporate structure and has thrown away too many of the key collective and collaborative characteristics of partnership, warts and all, will find itself doing anything quite as foolish as that.

The Limited Partnership (not to be confused with the 'Limited Liability Partnership') has been around for a while and is governed by the Limited Partnership Act 1907. This is in effect an old-style partnership with some limited partners in addition to the general partners, who continue to have unlimited liability. The liability of limited partners is limited only up to their capital commitment, in return for which safeguard they are not allowed to participate in the general management of the firm. This type of partnership has proved popular as a vehicle for investment funds in recent years.

Incorporated entities

Unincorporated entities, by and large, are entities that, in one sense, don't even exist – at least not separately from their founders. An incorporated entity, however, has a form that is recognised in law and is independent from its founders. An incorporated entity has an owner – someone who owns the capital or equity of the business. Given that most incorporated entities are set up to enable several individuals to share ownership, the owners of capital in such a business have become known – in the UK at least – as 'shareholders'. (In the USA they are more commonly called 'stockholders' and they own 'stock', not 'shares'.)

The joint stock limited liability incorporated company is the most common vehicle for owners to own a business with ambitions to grow in the UK. You can set one up in a few hours and on-line with a credit card if you already have a name for your company in mind and use the services of an agency to buy a company 'off the shelf'. A private company

'Getting consensus has been likened to trying to herd cats, but a good partnership will reach consensus in the end, which will significantly reduce the risk of individual partners doing daft things.'

(in contrast to a PLC) needs only one shareholder, and can get away with only one director as long as someone else is appointed as company secretary. Formation will require the drafting of a Memorandum and Articles of Association – the constitution of the company, governing matters such as name, objects, powers, shares, meetings and administration – but for many companies these documents are fairly standard, and they too can be bought on-line.

A company offers an owner the best chance of protecting his assets, and the best chance of raising finance. As a legal entity separate from its owners, a limited company can make contracts and it can be taken to court. It can raise money. It can be sold by its owners to other owners, or to another company or organisation, and thus has a continuing existence apart from its owners. It can even be sued by its owners. The owners of the business, the shareholders, can to a great extent hide behind the 'veil of incorporation' and restrict their liabilities to the amounts of money they have invested in the company's share capital. A company will often find it easier to do business than an unincorporated entity – easier to find customers and suppliers. Some organisations, and government agencies in particular, seem to have problems doing business with small, unincorporated entities. Some financiers will not provide finance unless the business is incorporated.

Limited liability is a powerful concept and at least reduces the risks inherent in business formation. But those risks are not eliminated; they are shared with others – financiers, customers, suppliers, employees and other stakeholders. A supplier offering goods on credit to a limited company in one sense carries more risk than a supplier to a partnership. If the company fails, the extent to which the supplier will get his money back is limited to the financial resources of the company. If the partnership fails, the supplier can pursue the individual partners. A company therefore has to pay for the privilege of limited liability, and the position of other stakeholders has to be protected. Compared to unincorporated entities, incorporated entities are subject to a lot of statute and regulation. A company has to file financial statements, and if the company is above a certain size it needs an audit. The relationship of directors to companies is more closely regulated than the relationship of partners to their partnerships. And, above all, companies and the people responsible for them need to be particularly careful if the company gets into trouble and starts dicing with insolvency. In such circumstances the

company's ability to carry on business becomes circum-
scribed. Directors who indulge in 'wrongful trading' run the
risk of personal liability, bans and the possibility of seeing the
'veil of incorporation' – the status of limited liability – lifted,
exposing the people behind the business as if they had been
involved in unlimited businesses. This area is covered in more
detail in the book in this series on finance directors.

Shareholder rights

Unlike the partnership or the sole trader, the limited company
has a clear distinction between ownership and management.
The fact that in small businesses many owners and managers
are owner-managers, and get confused in managers' meetings
about whether they are taking decisions as shareholders or as
managers, doesn't blur this difference. What gives an owner-
manager the right to manage a business is not her shareholding, though that obviously has considerable influence,
particularly if she has a controlling shareholding in the
company and can therefore dictate the composition of the
board. Her right to manage is established usually by the fact
that she is a director of the business. Unsurprisingly therefore
many investors will make a seat on the board a condition of
the deal.

The duties of directors are discussed in the other titles in
this series – particularly in the book on the role of the finance
director – but they have the effect of leaving the shareholder
in a very 'hands-off' role. Indeed, the primary duty even of
the directors is to the company, not to the individual shareholders. The distinction is fine, but important. Indicative of

the limited power of shareholders is the new right (from 2002) of shareholders in quoted companies to vote on directors' remuneration. The vote allows them to express a view on the remuneration, but doesn't allow them to control it.

The shareholder has a right to receive financial statements – or at least summary financial statements – and the right to inspect various registers and documents. Most shareholders will also have the right to attend and vote at company meetings, to receive dividends, and to transfer their shares to others – but these rights are often subject to restrictions in the

> '**[The private shareholder] from Fife** shamed Ms Swann [the new chief executive] into admitting that although she was given 141,000 shares in W. H. Smith when she joined in November, she had not spent any of her own cash on buying shares. "So she has no faith in the company?" [he] asked.' [From the meeting at which disgruntled W. H. Smith shareholders voted against the group's remuneration report, January 2004][1]

company's articles of association or shareholder agreements and are dependent on the type and class of share held. Most shareholders have the right to apply to a court for cancellation of a special resolution approving any payment out of capital for the redemption or purchase by a private company of its own shares – but this is as rare as it is obscure. These rights in total are fairly minimal. The only real power most shareholders have is the ability to sell their shares – which may focus the minds of directors of listed companies when done in sufficient numbers to threaten the share price, but may literally be more trouble than it is worth for the holder of a minority share in a private company. It is quite likely in any case to be limited by pre-emption rights in the articles.

All holders of the same class of shares are equal, but some are more equal than others. An owner of more than 50 per cent of voting shares in a company (a controlling majority shareholder) can, indirectly at least, dictate what a company does because he will – in the absence of any other constraints – control the board. The directors are voted in by the shareholders, and a majority shareholder will in effect be able to select who runs the company. Subject to the fact that a 75 per cent vote will be needed to pass special resolutions, he will therefore be in a position to dictate to minority shareholders, and the power of minority shareholders is very weak indeed by comparison.

Minorities with control over more than 25 per cent of the share capital will be able to block a special resolution, and will thus be able to influence decisions on matters such as:

- changing the company's name
- changing the memorandum or articles of association
- going public
- allowing the company to buy back its own shares and / or providing financial assistance for this
- voluntary solvent winding-up.

The holders of still smaller percentages of the shares also have some rights – assuming you have the time, the energy and the financial wherewithal to take your fellow shareholders through the courts. For example, a 15 per cent holding will

'All holders of the same class of shares are equal, but some are more equal than others.'

allow you to apply to a court to cancel a change to the objects clause in a memorandum of association – though most objects clauses are drafted very broadly in the first place.

Holders of 10 per cent of the shares may apply to a court to cancel a special resolution to provide financial assistance for the purchase of a company's own shares. They can also oblige the directors to call an extraordinary general meeting, and demand a poll of voting rights (rather than a show of hands) on any issue in a general meeting (other than the election of a chairman or the adjournment of a meeting). If particularly aggressive, a holder of 10 per cent has the right to apply to the Department of Trade to appoint an inspector to investigate the affairs of the company.

So it can be seen that most minority shareholders have little power or authority. What little they do have will require the expensive support of lawyers and courts to have any teeth, and any victory is likely to be Pyrrhic. Minority shareholder rights can therefore look like paper rights only, so it is particularly important that the position of a minority shareholder is

> **'Where stock is held** by a great number, what is anybody's business is nobody's business.'[2]

protected by way of a properly drafted shareholders' agreement. Without such an agreement, a minority shareholder is at the mercy of the majority shareholder, and in some ways is in a worse position than a partner in a partnership without a partnership agreement. Even though the affairs of the company should never be 'conducted in a manner which is unfairly prejudicial to the interests of its members generally or of some part of its members,'[3] self-interest is always a strong motivator, and a majority shareholder will have more of it than a minority shareholder. A shareholders' agreement will help the minority face up to the majority.

Minority shareholdings and valuation

A key issue for many though not all owners is the value of what they own. The directors of public companies always seem to believe that the market undervalues their companies. Private companies are very difficult to value in the first place. There is no open market for their shares, and the value of a private company is usually the negotiated price between the buyer and the seller, with neither being entirely happy, but both being happy enough to do the deal.

The value of a minority share of a private company is even more difficult, if that is all that's for sale. The value of the share may well be influenced by terms set out in the shareholder agreement (if it exists) or the articles of association, but these documents will often have more to say on the *process* of arriving at a value, or who is able to have first rights to buy the share (usually called 'pre-emption rights'), than on the value itself.

Usually the value itself, the 'fair value', as it is often referred to in the documentation, will be determined by an independent expert – usually a specialist accountant or corporate financier – who will firstly attempt to come up with a value for the business as a whole. He may well use a variety of techniques to derive a value or range of values from the business's past performance, future prospects or net assets, or the relative market values of similar businesses that have been bought and sold recently, or that are currently listed.

Secondly, the independent expert will tackle the vexed topic of the 'minority discount'. The value of the minority share is not simply determined by taking the value of the whole and allocating the minority a value proportionate to the extent of the holding, unless of course it's the whole of the business that's for sale. Unless the valuation basis set out in the Shareholders' Agreement and the Memorandum and Articles of Association indicates otherwise, the value of a minority holding will be discounted by a significant factor to account for the fact that the shareholding doesn't have control, and to reflect the lack of a market for the shares. And the discount per share can be significant – 60 per cent, 70 per cent or maybe even more, compared to the value of a share held by a majority shareholder.

Types of shareholder

It's not just the size of the holding that prevents all shareholders from being equal. There are different sorts of share, and shares of the same sort can be put into different classes with different rights.

Ordinary shares

These are common-or-garden shares. Ordinary shareholders carry the most risk in that they will rank after all other investors, particularly debt-holders. They will receive a dividend only after the others have had their demands satisfied, and if the business goes under it's only if there's anything left over after everyone else has been paid that they will get any capital back. On the other hand ordinary shareholders are most likely to be able to participate in any capital growth in the business. Many companies have different types of ordinary shareholder, and will classify their ordinary shares as type A or type B and so forth – typically for different shareholder groups. The types will carry different voting rights, or different rankings for profit participation.

Deferred shares

A share which ranks behind another when it comes to distributing profits is often called a 'deferred share'.

Founder shares

Shares owned by the founders of the business sometimes have special rights all of their own, and are often specially designated as 'founder shares'.

Preference shares

These are shares that rank ahead of ordinary shares for one reason or another. Often they will receive a right to a dividend before the ordinary shareholders, and they will rank ahead of ordinary shareholders when it comes to distributing capital on the winding up of the company. On the other hand, the dividend such shareholders receive is usually fixed – and is often expressed as a percentage of the nominal value of the share. And preferential shareholders usually don't receive a vote – except perhaps in circumstances where the dividend has not been paid – i.e. the company is 'in default'. A cynic might argue that preferential shareholders are debt holders in all but name and without any of the tax advantages (i.e. dividends are paid out of post-tax profits, whereas debt interest is paid out of pre-tax profits). But preference shares of one sort or another (or loan stock) are often used by financial investors as an element in a structured investment.

Participating preference shares

A preference share that might also carry some further right to participate in the profits – normally after the fixed dividend has been paid.

Cumulative preference shares

Most preference shares are of this type: if the company fails to pay the preference dividend one year, then the right to the dividend is not lost but is rolled-up into the next year. Ordinary shareholders, of course, do not benefit from this sort of luxury. But their dividends in good years might well be much better than those paid to preference shareholders with cumulative rights.

Redeemable shares

Shares which are issued on condition that they can be sold back to the company at a specified time in the future. They might or might not carry voting rights.

Convertible securities

Usually loan stock that might convert into one or other type of share at a future date when certain conditions are fulfilled or not. Again, often used by financial investors to enable them to have their cake and eat it.

	Sole trader	Partnership	Limited partnership	LLP	Franchise	Limited company
Formation	Very simple	No partnership agreement obligatory, but strongly advised	Partnership agreement obligatory; the partnership must be registered	Similar formation to limited company – no members' agreement obligatory, but strongly advised	Can be complicated	Some forms to fill out, people to appoint and administration fees to pay
Statutory framework	None specifically	Partnership Act, 1890	Limited Partnership Act, 1907	Limited Liability Partnerships Act, 2000; Limited Liability Regulations 2001	None specifically, but competition law may apply in UK	Companies Act, 1985, and subsequent emendations
Personal liability	Unlimited for the owner	Unlimited and joint and several for the partners	Unlimited for the general partners, limited for the limited partners	Members' liability limited	Depends on whether franchisees and franchisors are limited liability entities	Owners' (i.e. shareholders') liability limited
Ability to raise finance	Severely restricted	Restricted. Partnerships essentially financed by the partners and their personal ability to raise finance	Restricted, but often used as a vehicle to allow 'sleeping partners' to invest without incurring unlimited liabilities	Untried territory, but likely to be similar to partnership	Good way of tempting new entrants (franchisees) to put money in	Offers greatest variety of financing opportunities
Tax	Personal	Personal	Personal	Personal	Corporate if incorporated	Corporate
Status of business	Not legally separate from owner	Not legally separate from partners	Not legally separate from partners	Separate legal entity	Separate legal entity if incorporated	Separate legal entity
Financial disclosure	None	None	None, other than for capital contribution of limited partners	Must file details of members, salaries, financial statements	Same as company, if incorporated	Must file financial statements etc (though disclosure much less onerous for SMEs)
Restrictions on owners	None	None	Limited partners are not allowed to participate in management	None really – though 'designated' members have more administrative responsibilities than normal members	Depends on franchise agreement	Depends on nature and %age of shares held by 'owners' and whether they are directors or not.

Types of ownership structure

- Financier is not synonymous with owner
- The sole trader is the simplest form of ownership
- Partnerships come in an unlimited liability form and in two types of limited liability form
- Partners in a partnership are owners and financiers as well as managers
- A partnership agreement is imperative for a well-run partnership
- Incorporating the business as a limited liability company reduces the risks but doesn't eliminate them
- It's not shareholders that run companies, it's directors – though a majority shareholder can dictate who the directors are
- Not all shareholders are equal: minority shareholders do have some safeguards, but not many
- The value of a minority shareholding will be subject to a discount per share compared to the value of a majority shareholding
- Different shareholders have different rights. There may even be different classes of ordinary shareholder. Make sure you know which type you are

3

Growth stages

KEY TO THE experience of owning a growing business is an understanding of the nature of the beast that you own.

The most important characteristic of the growing business is the fact that it evolves as it gets bigger – it should grow up as it grows. There have been many attempts over the years to both describe and understand the nature of this evolution, and it is easy to see why. If you can understand the change then you can predict it. And if you can predict it then you can control it. Unfortunately things in business are never that simple. But just being able to understand the nature of the change is a huge step forward for many business owners, whose inability to deal with the change as it happens is an important constraint on the business and its capacity to grow.

The DIAMOND model

The DIAMOND growth model is one of many ways of illustrating some of the key transitions that growing businesses pass through. There are many similar attempts to describe what happens to businesses as they grow – stage-by-stage analytical descriptions of what happens to a business when it grows.

The DIAMOND growth model

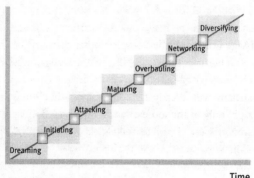

The fact that most of these models tell similar stories in different ways suggests that it is possible to make generalisations. They offer some useful insights to the owners of a growing business.

The DIAMOND model presents growth on a graph along two axes. The horizontal axis represents the passing of time. The vertical axis represents the size of a company. Growth can be measured in a number of different ways – by turnover, profit or number of employees. Most businesses know that they are growing not from the numbers but from the experience. Growth is a subjective experience. The entrepreneur may well get excited about top line growth. A finance director will be far more interested in growth in earnings. A capable human resources director will have a firm grip on increases in head count and increases in staff costs (and the relationship between the two). A business owner is more likely to be interested in the growth in value of the business. All of these versions of growth are right, but necessarily partial. Growth is really about all of them – which means that for many businesses it might be more useful to conceptualise growth as a passage from simple to complex rather than small to big.

As a business grows, it will pass through successive stages, each represented by a box on the graph. Fastidious mathematicians will already be complaining that this graph is a 'graph' only in the loosest sense. But the graph stands up to common sense if not mathematical scrutiny – which is the way most business people prefer it.

Passing from one stage to another is what change is all about. But businesses don't close on 31 December in one stage and open again on 1 January in another stage. Larry E. Greiner,[4] when putting together one of the first and best known of these 'growth models', suggested contrasting phases of gently changing evolution and crisis-ridden, high-pressure revolution. There's undoubtedly something in his distinction between the two types of growth, and the importance of the business's ability to cope with both.

DIAMOND suggests that the stages are divided, not necessarily by crises and revolutions, but by smoother, though still complex, transitions. As an organisation passes through each stage of growth, it carries with it cultural, organisational and administrative vestiges of its former self. These traces of an earlier phase in its development may prove beneficial, neutral or harmful. But it is impossible for an organisation to rid itself of their influence altogether. Just like people, organisations carry their history around with them. This has important implications when it comes to

'And you need them to be excited by change, because in moving from small to big, and from simple to complex, that is exactly what they are going to have to go through.'

considering how businesses pass from one stage to the next. At the very least a business will pass through a transitional phase. Much more common is for a business to experience the characteristics of two, or even three or more phases of growth simultaneously. The stages will be of different durations, and they will overlap.

When business owners try to think of their businesses in terms of DIAMOND, the realisation that they might be in several phases at once generates differing reactions. Some will probe deeper. Maybe their approach to employee management is less advanced than their approach to marketing, for example. For some this might trigger a line of thinking that will end in investment in HR strategy. For others the analysis will tell them what they already know, and reflect a strategic choice on the part of the organisation – and reconfirm them in their direction: a business that is sales and marketing led may be prepared to invest less in HR strategy as a price of its chosen strategy. Other owners might read into the analysis that various divisions of the business are in different stages of development. The internal-newsletter-publishing business may be less developed than the financial-reports-design business – after all, the former may be a relatively new venture. Expecting the two divisions to share the same characteristics could well do damage to both.

Expecting the business as a whole to sit in one stage only may be comforting to the tidy minded, but rarely reflects reality of growth. Nevertheless an understanding of the differing characteristics of each stage is useful.

Dreaming and initiating

The dreaming stage is what it says on the packet. It's what happens before the business is put together – before there's anything to own. A business in this stage isn't a business at all, of course. But pre-formation activity is nonetheless important to what happens afterwards. My colleague at

London Business School, John Mullins, has a whole book devoted to the stage, called *The New Business Road Test: What entrepreneurs and executives should do before writing a business plan*.

The defining qualities of entrepreneurs are discussed in the book in this series on finance directors; but entrepreneurship is all about the ability to get something done, and the wish to 'do it my way'. Entrepreneurship overlaps with the ability to invent, and also with the wish to get rich, but is different from both.

Entrepreneurship shares something with ownership as well. But though entrepreneurs do go into business to 'be the boss' and to 'do my own thing', they don't go into business to 'own' something. Successful entrepreneurs find themselves

> **'IBM was tough.** IBM came to our house – we had told them ahead of time that we worked out of our house. IBM had a policy against dealers who worked out of their homes. You had to have a storefront. They said, "We have to get approval about the house." '[5]

owning something almost as a by-product of their success. *Investors* in start-ups are far more likely to see themselves as would-be owners than the entrepreneur. This reflects the passive nature of ownership, compared to the active nature of entrepreneurship – but also suggests why entrepreneurs often make uncomfortable owners and why the question is often when rather than whether an entrepreneur should sell.

Given that the dreaming stage is all about entrepreneurship

rather than ownership, and is characteristic of a business that isn't there to be owned yet, you might be forgiven for questioning why we're wasting any time on it. But these pre-business formation stages are critical. Decisions taken before the business is founded have the most influence on the business after its formation, and are the most difficult to reverse. Perhaps the most important set of issues for the business founder to wrestle with at this stage relates to the extent and nature of his own ambition. How far do you want to grow? How much effort are you prepared to put in? And, of course, this matters hugely to the potential owner.

The initiating phase is about launching the business. It's about marshalling sufficient resources to deliver, and raising a sufficient amount of interest in the market to get the business off the ground.

The most useful tips for the new or future business owner are that – regardless of the quality of your planning – you will need more resources than you think, and raising interest will take much longer than you think.

At this stage immense pressure falls on to the business founder. There's some research to show that businesses founded by teams tend to grow faster and bigger than businesses founded by individuals. A team can spread the load and play to the strengths of its individual members. For the one-man business, recruiting that first new member of staff is a critical decision, because the individual you recruit will disproportionately influence the direction of the business in its early stages. This is discussed in much more detail in the books on the finance director and the managing director in this series.

In the initiating stage it's a bit much to talk of a business as something that an owner owns. The business plan will look expensive, and might actually have cost a lot to produce, but it won't be worth anything. A new business will rarely be cash positive. If there are new employees they will consider themselves lucky to be paid at all, and even luckier to be paid next month as well. Their time horizons won't be any longer than

> **'In this early stage** ... the main problems of the business are obtaining customers and delivering the product or service contracted for... The owner is the business, performs all the important tasks, and is the major supplier of energy, direction and, with relatives and friends, capital.'[6]

that. The business won't be sustainable – and it is not severable from the interests of the founder. The founder will live and breathe the business – but in great part this is because the business won't be able to live and breathe for itself.

But some key ownership decisions will already have been taken. Has the business been incorporated? Or is it trading as a partnership, or maybe even a limited liability partnership? Where is the funding coming from? How much of it is debt and how much equity?

Attacking

The business opportunity has been demonstrated. The business has turned cash-positive. It may already be delivering a decent return to its founding owners. It will be keen to be taken seriously by the outside world – it may, for example, try

'What is really at stake here is not so much the pace of growth, but whether the growth is controlled or not.'

to appear bigger and grander than it actually is. It may have registered for VAT before reaching the relevant threshold; it may have taken advantage of the internet to create an impression on the web that belies the actual scale of the business; it may have registered as a PLC, even though there's no intention of listing the shares on a stock market. But, although the business looks as if it could have a life of its own, its fortunes are still tied up with those of its founders, and it's still too early to let it out of the pouch.

Selling and salesmanship are key skills – indeed, many businesses at this stage seem to survive on salesmanship alone. But
the truth is that the business has begun to establish some of
the systems necessary to survive and reach the goal of self-
sustainability, and the first signs of real tension between the

---

'The image of the entrepreneur as a great inventor and great
promoter or the great and daring risk-taker simply doesn't
square with the facts. Reality is far less spectacular than this.
In fact in the beginning entrepreneurship turns out to be a
mundane affair and not at all heroic. There is the entrepreneur
without capital source, without apparent social skills, and
without even a good idea. No respectable element in the
community is even aware of him, let alone ready to help him.'[7]

---

owner and the manager are appearing. For the owner-
manager this will mean sleepless nights.

The instinctive reaction of some owners may be to slow
down business growth. Isn't the ability of the business to generate cash enough? Haven't I put enough long hours into this
business already? Isn't it time to spend more time with my
children? For most owners the peace of mind they think
slowing down might bring is illusory. A business that loses
confidence and ambition in this stage will be a business that
stays perpetually fragile. What is really at stake here is not so
much the pace of growth, but whether the growth is controlled or not. For the first time the founders have to invest in
systems and controls that look after the interests of the business rather than just the interests of the founders.

With business systems and controls the first thing is to recognise that you need them, and the second is to realise that you are probably going to have to throw them away next year because you will have outgrown them. Systems must be flexible to have any life at all. And flexible usually means simple as well.

Maturing

This stage is all about building an effective, professional, disciplined management structure that knows what's going on in the business, and is aware of what might be on the horizon.

Building a professional team is difficult. You want people who know how to run a sizeable business, because that is what you are trying to build. But at the same time they need to be in sympathy with the demands of running a smaller business because that is what you've got. And you need them to be excited by change, because in moving from small to big, and from simple to complex, that is exactly what they are going to have to go through.

Building a professional team is about changing the approach of the founders too. Maturing is about growing up as well as just growing. It's about running a management team as if they are adults rather than children. It's about having a business that is set up to run itself with the appropriate checks, balances and warning lights, rather than one that is run by sheer force of personality. Many founders find that this stage is also about giving up control for the first time. Not only is the agenda of the business now firmly established, and separately defined from the personal agendas of the

'For the first time the founders really are beginning to experience what it is like to be owners.'

founders – but the various business and personal agendas are beginning to do each other damage. For the first time the founders really are beginning to experience what it is like to be owners.

Supporting future growth, and in particular financing future growth, may well involve inviting others to participate in ownership. Indeed, giving equity away may be a necessary aspect of raising capital for funding business expansion. But giving a measure of ownership away is part of being grown up about delegation and management. How ownership is shared will itself be influenced by the structure and form of the organisation to start off with. Inviting someone to become an equity partner has a different feel and gives different messages from inviting him to have some equity or an option over equity, or inviting him to become a franchisee. It has different legal implications as well. Ownership becomes tied up with questions of remuneration, reward, motivation and incentive. For the first time it may also force on to the discussion table the eventual exit of the founder. One of the defining characteristics of an owner is the ability to talk sensibly about selling up.

Overhauling

Maturing is all about the business growing up. Overhauling is about making sure premature ageing doesn't set in. It is almost inevitable that a business will 'overdo it' in the maturing phase, and that some sort of correction will be necessary in the overhauling stage. Indeed, this overdoing and correcting is an important learning experience in the life cycle of the growing business.

Entrepreneurs and professional managers are key to business formation and development, but that doesn't mean they see eye to eye. Entrepreneurs often found businesses so they can escape from the constraints of a big business. They find it a shock to discover that they have created just the sort of business they wanted to escape from in the first place. On the other hand, it is naive to assume a complex business can develop successfully without management discipline. Overhauling the organisation is not about taking the business

> **'When you're growing this quickly** every day is a new day. Every day we worry that we've never been this size before, and we worry that we've missed something new.'

back; it is about achieving balance between the entrepreneurial spirit and the managerial discipline. The business is more competitive and has a strong customer and marketing orientation, but there is a sense of missed opportunity and a consequent drive to optimise performance. A focus on performance management is often characteristic of this stage as the business attempts to rediscover a spirit of enterprise, with teams and individuals often held accountable for results and offered appropriate incentives.

If exit strategies first get aired in the maturing stage, an actual exit is a common phenomenon in the overhauling stage. No role changes more than that of the founder as the business evolves, and it is a rare individual indeed who can steer a business successfully through all seven stages of DIAMOND. The fact that a few do – and consequently get a lot of national press coverage – does not fool those who know about growth into forgetting that such individuals are the exceptions that prove the rule. Indeed, many founders have stayed on too long and damaged their businesses and their fortunes. The rule is that the founder *will* and should seek an exit, and it is a question not of whether but of when.

A business without its founder is a business without the personality that has got it this far. This is where organisational culture, brand and organisational values start to become important, as they fill the gap vacated by the personality of the founder. Culture, brand and values, unlike personality, are artificial constructs and need to be managed. The business owner, on the other hand will have a personality – but his personality no longer has anything to do with the business he has an interest in. Brand often gets attention first in the growing, entrepreneurial business, focused on its relationships with its clients and customers. Ultimately, businesses don't have a choice as to whether they should have a brand or not. But it's their choice whether to manage it or not.

Networking and diversifying

Rather than analysing two further, sequential stages of organisational development, the last two stages in the DIAMOND model explore different aspects of the mature, sustainable, professionally managed business.

A business in the networking stage of the model now has a life independent from its founders and its owners. It is more probable that the business conceives of itself as a network of businesses rather than as one. Strategic processes have

'This is where organisational culture, brand and organisational values start to become important, as they fill the gap vacated by the personality of the founder.'

become as important as tactical ones and business planning processes need to reflect this.

In the maturing and overhauling stages, brand begins to take over from the personality of the founder as a defining and controlling influence in the business, and is the subject of serious investment. After brand, organisational culture and internal values receive attention, with outside consultants paid to help the business define and manage what it used to take for granted. If brand is the way that culture manifests itself to the outside world, culture and values are the way the brand lives inside the organisation.

Maintaining and developing a corporate image internally and externally is therefore important, as by now the business is being managed for the benefit of a diverse stakeholder group. The business has a significant impact on its environment as employer, property owner, consumer and producer.

> **'Henry Ford's determination** to manage the whole of his business empire personally was legendary, notwithstanding the fact that its increasing scale made this impossible. He had no patience with management theory and let it be known that anyone found with an organisation chart, however sketchily drawn, would be sacked on the spot.'[8]

Businesses need to take their responsibilities to outside stakeholders seriously if they haven't done so already, and they have to be capable of withstanding external scrutiny.

Under the heading of diversifying, developing relationships with other organisations as partners might well come to the fore as the business explores strategic alliances and opportunities up and down the business chain. The culture of organisations in this stage is highly focused and is managed in a sophisticated way using brand, corporate strategy and communication. In this stage it is too easy to assume that growth will slow. It may, but it needn't. Significant growth will probably be the result of fundamentally new initiatives rather than a consequence of developments in the core businesses. Mergers and acquisitions are likely to be much talked about if they have not been before.

Businesses in this stage are complex, sophisticated organisations. The significant majority will be sizeable concerns. Those managers and directors who have been with the business since inception – if there are any – will have seen the business change out of all recognition several times.

Is diversification the end of the road for the growing business? Of course not. By the time a business gets to this stage it often sees itself as a portfolio of businesses. With this in mind, some business managers prefer to see various parts of their increasingly diversified business empires as having different DIAMOND models of their own.

The reality of growth is that the whole cycle may be seen to start again, with people extracting themselves from big business (or being delegated within a big business) to start a new growing business from scratch.

The DIAMOND model is essentially a linear model describing a linear process – it starts bottom left, and ends up top right. But what happens then? Of course, to suggest that a growing business has no future once it has reached the end of the model is nonsense. However, although many businesses find it easiest to think of themselves in linear terms despite the 'what happens next?' question, some prefer to describe business growth as a circular process. Inherent in the later stages of business development is a need to reinvent the business, to generate new businesses from the old one. This can be conceptualised as the model starting again – symbolised by the last stage containing within it smaller versions of the model as a whole.

- Businesses change as they grow
- It is possible to generalise about the sorts of change a business will go through as it grows
- There's no tidy passing from one stage of development to another
- Different parts of the business can be in different stages of development
- No role changes more than that of the founder as the business grows

4

Sharing ownership with others

As with every other element in business, ownership is not static. An ambitious, growing business will want and need to change its ownership structure if it wishes to maximise its chance of growing and changing. Ultimately, owners will sell; but in the shorter term a business will benefit from inviting more individuals into the business as owners.

Franchising

A franchise is not an independent legal form, but a way of structuring the business that facilitates sharing of ownership. A typical franchise will involve a franchiser, a franchise agreement and franchisees. The franchiser will own the rights to key elements of the business model – the brand, the name, the patents or know-how. The franchiser will allow the franchisee the right to use the brand, the name and so forth, in order to set up a satellite site. The franchise agreement will govern how the franchisee will run her business, and also the role of the franchiser. The franchiser, in addition to selecting the franchisees, will provide them with training and other resources including national advertising and marketing materials. The franchisee will pay the franchiser, of course – all franchises are different, but there will usually be an up-front sum to pay, and an on-going charge based on turnover or profits. Franchisees will have other costs to bear, of course. But the franchiser may be able to help them towards sources of finance, and other pooled resources to keep operating costs lower.

> **'As an owner-manager** I've learned never to underestimate people's capacity to be selfish.'

When the fees are paid and the terms met, the franchisee will own her franchise, and the franchiser will continue to own rights to, and have a continuing influence over, the intellectual property behind the business. And there will be circumstances in which the franchiser can withdraw the franchise.

A franchise structure is an excellent way of rolling out a replicable business. It is a way of inviting in new owners and sourcing new capital. The franchisee will be able to own a business whilst being protected from many of the risks of business start-up. It is also a good way of rolling out fast. If you are interested in securing the benefits of first mover advantage then franchising may help you reach the scale needed in the necessary timeframe. Obviously some businesses are better suited to franchising than others. Retail outlets are often franchises – with Body Shop (in its early years at least) and McDonalds being high-profile examples.

Some founder-owners see franchising as a route towards losing control. Founders often worry that franchising risks

'A franchise structure is an excellent way of rolling out a replicable business.'

compromising quality and consistency. But this is incorrect. It's growth, not franchising, that presents the greatest challenge to an owner's ability to control her business, and to a business's consistency and quality. Franchising offers one way of attempting to control a business as it grows. Whether it works or not as a control mechanism is down to the quality of the franchise agreement, the quality of the people behind the business, and the quality of those recruited to the business as franchisees. As always with growth, it's about people.

Franchising is not a formal legal structure, and it may well incorporate different forms of structure within it. But, most commonly, a franchisee will incorporate her particular franchise as a company.

Sharing ownership in partnerships

Franchising offers one mechanism for sharing ownership with new people. There are others.

The sustainability of a partnership will depend on its ability to attract new talent – not just to the firm, but to the rank of partner as well. A partner is not the same thing as a shareholder in a company; but as an owner of the business, a partner has a share of something of value. But she will not be able to realise capital value unless there are new partners coming in to acquire her stake, or unless the whole business is sold. In practical terms, the value of the partnership represented by the partner will be lost when the partner retires unless there's someone else to take the reins. In financial terms, a partner will not be able to convert her capital into cash unless others are prepared to put cash in. Promotion to partnership is therefore much more than a promotion; as an admission to ownership it is much more difficult than a recruitment exercise. It is about finance and it is about the commercial sustainability of the practice. A well-managed partnership will keep a careful eye on the age range and average age of the partnership – both are key indicators of the long-term health of the business.

A decision that is difficult for the partnership should also be difficult for the individual. Although the partnerships involved usually consider the matter to be a personal insult, there are many individuals who have turned down an invitation to join the partnership because they have been nervous about the ownership and financial responsibilities that go with the job. The fact that a move into the partnership involves giving up employment rights and assuming unlimited liability (unless you're joining a limited liability partnership) further complicates the decision for the individual.

Sharing ownership in companies

Companies have tended to make more of a song and dance about 'admission' to ownership than to partnerships, even though much more is at stake in partnerships. By and large my experience suggests that partnerships should work harder at their partner admission procedures and companies should be a little less precious about sharing ownership – as long as they have found an individual who has potential as an *owner*. Of course, it's not a company that shares ownership, it's a shareholder. An individual who controls a limited company is not going to be as predisposed to sharing ownership as a partner in a partnership. Partnership is, after all, by definition a collective enterprise. Nevertheless, a shareholder who is dogmatic about refusing to sell shares to someone else may be adding to the constraints on growth. The owners are the ultimate source of capital in a business, including finance, but they are much more than this. As the source of capital, the owners are the ultimate source of culture, values and strategic thinking. All businesses need more of all these as they grow and develop.

In recent years it has been fashionable to look for ways of 'aligning' the interests of other stakeholders with the interests of shareholders. It was once rare for directors to have equity, but it is now rare for them not to be so honoured – or at least to not be treated to an option over equity. But there is a difference between being 'aligned' with the interests of the owners, and feeling, thinking and acting like an owner.

In the UK, the Chancellor has worked hard to offer incentives – usually tax breaks – to those prepared to 'invest' in smaller businesses and to owner-managers. This has confused people. Too many individuals are minded to invest to cut their tax bills rather than focusing on the concerns of the business – witness the distress that results when small investors have congratulated themselves on saving tax by investing in equity-based savings arrangements, only to find a year later that their investment is worth a lot less than when they started. Very few of those investing in these sort of vehicles see themselves as owners, even if equity is at the heart of their investment vehicle.

Tax is the cart, not the horse, and a potential shareholder in any business, big or small, should never forget which comes first. A business should not assume that a shareholder encouraged to invest by a tax scheme will have his priorities right – in fact it would be safer to assume the opposite. You don't want your investors' decisions to be driven by tax considera-

> **'If you want managers to act** in their shareholders' best interests, take away their company stock.'[9]

tions. Fancy tax planning may look good on paper, and may work wonders for your tax position, but circumstances change, and a business wishing to unpick an arrangement may find that existing investors risk losing their tax benefits. In general terms, the more generous the incentives offered by

'Tax is the cart, not the horse, and a potential shareholder in any business, big or small, should never forget which comes first.'

the Chancellor to businesses and individuals, the more onerous will be the conditions that need to be fulfilled – and maintained – to earn them. A good example is the much-commented-on Enterprise Management Incentive (EMI) share options scheme. This is designed to give employees the right to buy shares at a preferential price at a date in the future, without incurring an income tax liability when the option is granted or exercised or the shares sold; and with capital gains tax taper relief running from the date the options were granted rather than the date they are exercised. But the scheme comes with a set of 'disqualifying events'. These include the business becoming the 51 per cent subsidiary of another company, or no longer carrying on a 'qualifying trade', the definition of which excludes finance or property and also business not carried out wholly or mainly in the UK. Some of these disqualifying events are real threats to the business with ambitions to grow – and a threat might well turn into an actual barrier to growth if the business is not careful. A business that loses its eligibility for EMI would run the risk of its EMI member employees incurring an income tax charge when they exercise their options – in addition to losing the tax benefits that attracted them in the first place.

It's not just tax that muddies the motivation of the would-be business owner. Some are inclined to confuse the role of *investor* with their role as owner. Someone wanting to encourage others to take a shareholding in an owner-managed busi-

> **'Options became just another form of currency,** rather than an incentive to own shares.'[10]

ness should not sell the arrangement as a get-rich scheme. Owner-managed businesses are inherently risky investments. If you are investing in the business you are working in, you risk putting too many eggs in one basket. In the USA it has been common for company pension schemes to invest in the company as well. Regulators have run the risk of exacerbating the situation further by allowing private companies and their advisers to invent structures, usually involving trusts, that create a degree of liquidity for their shares. Employee Share Ownership Trusts (ESOTs) allow shareholders in private companies the illusion that they are investing in something more akin to publicly traded shares than they really are. Individual shareholders are encouraged to think of themselves as

investors rather than owners. But if it's *just* the investment
return you're after, put it somewhere else. It's a dangerous
game to encourage employees to acquire shares in the business on the chance of making a fortune. (For a list of other
types of staff equity plans, see the 'Useful information'
chapter at the end of this book.)

Hence the popularity of options, which offer individuals
the opportunity of participating in the upside whilst minimis-
ing the up-front cash investment. Giving options to managers
has been much commented on in recent years – but usually
only in the context of the big listed company and the over-

> **'WorldCom's stock option plans** provide the means through
> which executive officers can build an investment in our
> common stock which will align such officers' economic
> interests with the interests of shareholders. Historically, the
> Committee has believed that the grant of stock options has
> been a particularly important component of its success in
> retaining talented management employees ...' WorldCom
> Remuneration Committee report

paid, super-rich chief executive. In addition to receiving out-
rageous salaries, executives have received options packages
designed to deliver ridiculous sums of money at predetermined future dates. (In a wonderful attempt to justify the
unjustifiable, it has been argued that executives will undervalue options in their own business – because as sophisticated
investors they will appreciate that they are not properly diversified – and thus will need to be awarded even more to be

properly motivated.)[11] In big listed companies, share options are just the thin end of a wedge of increasingly sophisticated financial instruments that blur the boundaries of ownership and debt, investment and income. The full range of these sophisticated instruments that have distorted the performance and measurement of listed companies and capital markets in recent years has not really hit private companies yet, but it is only a question of time. Already in some owner-managed businesses, options have led to further confused thinking amongst owners and employees.

Share options are often given to senior managers in entrepreneurial owner-managed start-ups to help compensate for the business's inability to pay a proper salary. Share options can indeed be a very useful instrument for motivating and rewarding staff in the young, growing business. But don't be fooled into thinking that someone turned on by options in these circumstances is necessarily thinking like a real owner. There's a big difference between a founder who commits his own cash, and someone who joins the owner shortly after, tempted by options. A manager who is given options in lieu of a decent salary is in effect being given deferred salary, not deferred equity. He's another manifestation of the debt-masquerading-as-equity syndrome.

In recent years the water has been muddied still further by accounting treatment. Companies have not had to account for options in the profit and loss account, arguing that the issue of an option is not a transfer of real value. Companies have, in other words, had further reason for pushing options at their staff. The attitudes of the accounting regulators are changing – but meanwhile, options have become very popular. Ten

'It's a dangerous game to encourage employees to acquire shares in the business on the chance of making a fortune.'

million employees got options in the USA in 2000, compared to fewer than one million in 1990 – and the pattern is by no means dissimilar in the UK. The accounting treatment that has contributed to this is more logical than it is sensible – presumably most of the ten million with options believe they are receiving something of value, even if the accounting authorities do not.

A word of qualification, lest it be inferred that I think widening share ownership is a bad idea. An owner-managed business serious about growth will need to invite more individuals to participate in ownership. If it doesn't, it will risk running short of ideas, energy, vision, values, innovation, culture and all the other intangible forms of capital that a business needs – even if it is lucky enough to be able to find its own financial resources. Options, tax incentives and trust mechanisms offer businesses new routes towards broadening

> **'Incentives consist of stock options** and cash awards paid to the company's senior and middle management executives. Mr McKelvey [CEO and founder] does not receive incentives.' TMP Worldwide; now Monster

ownership that can be cost effective and efficient. They can also provide highly effective mechanisms for incentivising and motivating staff. But a business exploring these routes needs to be very careful and take high-quality advice – not just on the tax issues but also on the longer-term consequences for the structure of the business, the motivation of the key people within it, and its ability to react to those future events, planned and unplanned, that will otherwise turn opportunities into obstacles.

Joint ventures and alliances

A few words are needed on joint ventures and alliances – because many of the perceived purposes in having new shareholders or partners may also be achieved by arrangements that don't alter the underlying ownership structure of the original business.

The labels 'joint venture' and 'alliance' are only two of several applied to a huge variety of arrangements between different businesses to exploit opportunities to their mutual advantage. These arrangements vary in form and function, in the degree to which they assume a legal form, and the extent to which they consume management time, finance and other resources.

Some joint ventures involve the creation of a separate business – sometimes even a new company that is jointly owned by the parties to the venture. But one of the key characteristics of a joint venture is that it rarely threatens the ownership of the joint venture partners themselves. The 'partners' to a joint venture can always retreat back to their own businesses where the pulls of ownership are strongest and most real. This has advantages and drawbacks. On the one hand an owner can protect his business both from a degree of commercial risk, and also from the inquisitive eyes of his joint venture partner. On the other hand it is notoriously difficult to summon up real commitment to the venture. Saying it's a good deal in the press statement is different from delivering the required commitment and energy – the sort of stuff that usually requires real ownership to muster.

Much of the value that is derived from joint ventures comes not from the official, costed and reported objectives of the venture, but from the unofficial, unplanned activities that inevitably come along with the package, and which are usually difficult to value or cost anyway.

- Franchising is an excellent way of rolling out a replicable business fast – if done well
- Franchising is all about the quality of the franchise agreement and the people recruited as franchisees
- In partnerships, the admission of a new partner is a big commitment – for the partner as well as the partnership. It isn't just a recruitment or a promotion exercise
- Don't let tax planning drive your ownership, recruitment or incentive decisions – or even your investment decisions
- Tax-effective share schemes always come at a cost
- Share options and share schemes can work well – but comprehensive and expert advice is essential
- Joint venture arrangements can be entered into without threatening ownership structures

5

Getting Out

THE PREVIOUS CHAPTER discusses some of the issues related to inviting new people to own the business. But for most owners – and particularly founder-owners – there will come a time to sell out altogether. Successful entrepreneurs, in possession of a thriving business, are often far more turned on by the excitement of buying someone else's business than they are by the prospect of selling their own. But for most these priorities need to be reversed. The fact that most entrepreneurs don't reverse these priorities explains why most business acquisitions subsequently fail to justify their acquisition price.

Selling can be difficult, particularly if you founded the business and watched it grow and develop in your ownership. If your business is buying and selling businesses you will feel differently – but you will be thinking more like a financier than an owner. For many owners, selling the business has been likened to selling the children. Unsurprisingly too many business owners leave it until too late and find themselves being yet another barrier to the business's growth and development. To the wise owner it's a critical rite of passage for the business – and it's an important rite of passage for the owner too.

Listing on the stock market

When the stock market is booming, the endgame many owners talk about is a listing on the stock market. It isn't necessarily an exit at all, of course – indeed owners will be locked in as owners (if not employees) for a period of time in many situations after the listing (particularly a listing on the alternative investment market, or AIM), and only the financial institutions will see the listing as an immediate exit. An initial public offering to the market (or 'IPO') is about admitting new owners rather than exiting existing ones – though admittedly an IPO is seen as an exit route for many. For those who stay, the relationship with the new business will be much changed. Public companies are not so much owned as

> **'Having been through an acquisition,** I now have my own league table of advisers. At the top I'd put those who really understand people. At the bottom I'd put strategy consultants.'

invested in. Though run for the shareholders, and in theory controlled by them, public companies are in effect controlled by directors who have often run the businesses for themselves. A director of a listed public company, even if armed with options and equity, is not an owner-manager, nor is he necessarily aligned with the interests of the shareholders, many of whom are now big institutional investors who need reporting to and whose expectations need massaging and then meeting. The owner-manager who continues to think, feel and act like an owner-manager after flotation will damage his business. Not that the business is really 'his' any more anyway.

For some, an IPO is not the great experience it is cracked up to be in the war stories. An IPO is very expensive. You'll need a sponsor – usually a merchant bank or a stockbroker – to advise on the share issue methodology, the issue price, the timing and the prospectus, which will be written with legal and accounting input. You'll need a broker to underwrite the flotation itself in case the issue is not taken up by the public or the institutions. You'll also need the broker to market the issue to institutions. And then there are accountants and solicitors, who in addition to their input on the share prospectus, will get involved with due diligence. The business will need to be 'groomed'. The management team will need to be dressed up (and an entrepreneur may find the new arrangements uncomfortable), and non-execs able to ensure the implementation of new corporate governance processes will need to be found. The whole process will take time – quite possibly up to two years. Costs vary, of course, but a recent survey suggests that costs of 10 per cent to 20 per cent of money raised[12] are not uncommon. For smaller businesses the percentage costs may well be even higher. But, big or small, by the end of the process the business will be very different from the one that went into the process.

The alternative investment market is an easier and cheaper route to the public markets. AIM companies can also be invested in through enterprise initiative schemes and venture capital trusts – unlike companies with full market listings. Regulatory costs are lower. But the price paid for this is less liquidity in the shares.

'Big or small, by the end of the process the business will be very different from the one that went into it.'

The flotation is the beginning, not the end. There are further annual costs involved in maintaining a listing – a recent study puts these at between 0.25 per cent and 0.35 per cent of the funds raised.[13] And then there is the time and energy cost involved in running a public business. Those

wondering whether it is worth it often have their concerns
exacerbated when they realise that the stock markets frequently undervalue smaller public companies. Indeed, despite

> **'Once we grew the company quite quickly,** then the job ...
> became a different animal. I was absolutely fed up with the
> City – a complete waste of time! They are not interested in
> strategy, only in our numbers...'[14]

the flotation, the shares may continue to be relatively illiquid,
leaving the owner feeling even more locked in. It is a rare individual who has been turned on by the excitement of founding
and running his own business who then goes on to succeed at
and enjoy the experience of directing a public business. Many
who make the transition will leave soon after the deal, or
move to non-executive status. Some, famously, want to take
their business back into private ownership some time later.
Tom Singh and clothing retailer New Look is a case in point.
Founded by Singh as a single shop in 1969, New Look made
the newspapers in early 2004 when it was announced that
Singh had found backing to take the business back into
private ownership. When New Look was originally floated in
1998, Singh – though still a significant shareholder – had
stepped back from active management, becoming a non-executive and a consultant. In 2004, amid the usual stories of the
business being undervalued by the market and of poor business performance, it was reported that, as part of the public-
to-private plans, Singh was to return to active management as
managing director.

A trade sale

The truth, of course, is that not many actually get to float their businesses in the first place. The IPO usually gets no further than a paragraph or two in the dreamy pages of an early business plan or an MBA student's case-study notes. The most common routes to exit for owner-managers lie elsewhere.

The simplest form of exit for an owner is the sale of the business to a third party, or 'trade sale'. But all exit transactions are complicated, and even the simplest is fraught with technical choices. Finding someone to buy the business is far from straightforward. The purchaser may be another individual, or another organisation – or, increasingly, 'financial buyers' such as specialist private equity institutions. Of course, many businesses don't know that they're for sale to start off with. An approach from another business or team tentatively enquiring whether you might be interested in selling will initially be flattering, but it can be one of the most destabilising events in a business's history. A focused management team leading a successful growing business can be torn apart as an offer to buy tests the differences between individual aspirations and ambitions.

Businesses that want to put themselves up for sale are hardly in an easier situation. Many businesses don't want to put up a 'For Sale' sign for fear of the messages it will send to customers and the competition, and the damage it will do to the business as a result. Even big businesses, relatively accustomed to buying and selling bits of themselves, are often very nervous about information relating to the sale of a division or

'An approach from another business or team tentatively enquiring whether you might be interested in selling will initially be flattering, but it can be one of the most destabilising events in a business's history.'

subsidiary getting out too fast or into the wrong hands. Some refuse to sell to competitors; others refuse to sell to management – even though both are potential purchasers and may be prepared to pay good prices. But a competitor who knows you are for sale may have a different strategy and may wish to do something else with their money at your expense. A management team that knows the business is for sale may become demotivated rather than excited. Alternatively they may see this as an opportunity to buy the business themselves. Control of information, as so often, is the key.

An owner looking for potential purchasers should not forget that he is not the only one looking for 'deal flow'. Accountants, lawyers, bankers and other financiers are also on the lookout and are often aware of potential candidates for the other side of your transaction. A discreet chat with one of your favoured professional advisers may often find you a worthwhile contact.

You will have to get professionals involved anyway. The transaction, regardless of its form, will be governed by complex contractual documentation, which must be written by and reviewed by professionals who know what they are doing. Finding such individuals is more difficult than it seems. Lawyers are good at contracts, of course – but they aren't always good when it comes to accounting practice and regulation, which can be critical in drafting key clauses. Accounting is the language of business, which is what will be used to describe precisely what is being bought and sold. Inexpert drafting leads to ambiguity which will result in post-deal disputes and further expense. You'll probably need both lawyers and accountants who are used to the sort of problems you are presenting them with – and in particular someone who is experienced in the documentation that governs business transfers. You don't want to be one of the big mistakes that professionals will tell you they learned most from. Indeed, your lead corporate finance adviser – probably an accountant – will have a key role in the success of the transaction: finding potential buyers, providing distance between the seller and the buyer, leveraging up the price, negotiating the commercial terms, managing the process, and transacting the deal.

Tax, as always, serves to complicate the issue still further. The sale of a successful business which a founder has built from scratch is likely to represent a significant capital gain. Fortunately, the capital gains tax regime in the UK at least is relatively generous, with an effective CGT rate down to 10 per cent after just two years of ownership in certain circumstances – but you will need expert advice to position your business appropriately and ensure that the right circumstances apply to you. It's certainly not the sort of thing that can be left to the final negotiation meeting, let alone to the time you deal with your tax returns after the business has been sold. For example, a trading company that over-indulges in certain activities (such as property) or which has too much surplus cash may compromise its ability to benefit from the most beneficial tax arrangements. With good advice in good time and a bit of advance planning these issues can often be addressed.

Then there is the matter of exactly what you are selling. Are you selling the company (i.e. the shares) or are you selling the trade and assets of the business? Selling the company as a whole is a tidier farewell, but there may be advantages to selling the assets of the company – in particular there may be tax advantages for a purchaser keen to obtain a corporate tax deduction for purchased goodwill and intellectual capital. A vendor should never forget that the sale of his business will depend upon the willingness of the purchaser, and the structure of the deal will have to suit both parties. Too often a sale is treated as a negotiation between two enemies. But the most successful transactions are always win-win situations for both sides.

Employee share schemes, option schemes and arrangements to offer tax incentives to existing owners and investors complicate matters as well. These may need transferring or unpicking – without risking the tax positions of the stakeholders.

Many deals involving the sale of an owner-managed business also involve an 'earn-out'. An earn-out is a deal in which the purchaser pays for the business in instalments, with the later instalments dependent on the success of the business – its achievement of targets. Typically this is a way of bridging a

> **'There was not one of them then present** who had not after some fashion been given to understand that his fortune was to be made, not by the construction of the railway, but by the floating of the railway shares.' Anthony Trollope, *The Way We Live Now*

price gap on negotiation and enabling the price to reflect extra value if forecasts are met. At first glance this looks like an excellent mechanism for the purchaser to manage at least some of the risks inherent in his investment decision, particularly in a 'people' business. If the business doesn't live up to the prospectus then he won't have to pay the full price. Conversely, an earn-out may be a way for a vendor to get a better price for his business. But the fact that many of these arrangements are at the heart of subsequent disputes between the purchaser and the vendor suggests that earn-out arrangements are very difficult to get right. Problems with definitions are common. Earn-outs are particularly problematic where the vendors continue working in the business for a period of time – which is usually the case, as earn-outs are often also seen as a way of motivating a vendor over a key transitional period. While the

> **'You shouldn't go into a major transaction** unless you are prepared to let your senior management team focus on nothing else for months on end.'

vendor is motivated to do whatever he can to maximise his earn-out, the new owner is keen to step in and control his new acquisition. Here lies the potential for a nasty conflict. It's very easy for the vendor to blame his failure to achieve his earn-out targets on the meddling of the new owner – who can be accused of having a good motive for ensuring that the vendor misses his targets, thus saving himself the expense of handing over the last instalments.

Management buy-outs

An MBO is a commonly used acronym given to an arrangement in which the current owners sell the business to the current managers. An MBO has a lot to recommend itself to owners as a means of selling out and turning their efforts into cash. The acquirers are known quantities and have a track record with the business which will be useful when trying to

'There will be many complex tax issues to consider.'

find finance. An MBO can be a mechanism for enabling the sale of a separable part of a business – a profitable subsidiary from an unsuccessful parent company, for example, or a non-core business being disposed of as a consequence of a change in group strategy. Given that an MBO is a deal that is essentially 'kept in the family' it is much easier to keep confidential than a trade sale. All business transfers are disruptive, but an MBO is more likely to allow the business to carry on as usual than a transfer that introduces entirely new owners to the business – although, once they get the sniff of an MBO, a management team may become dysfunctional as they attempt to position themselves and the business in a way that serves the interests of the deal. Indeed, it is vital that a potential MBO team take advice early: a mishandled management approach could lead to summary dismissal! An MBO team will need to have permission to explore the opportunity to avoid any breaches of fiduciary duty. A management team in this situation is going to suffer some of the symptoms of

> **'The culture is a big difference,** particularly for an owner-manager business where they may have a dominant individual who is used to doing what he wants to, has his car on the books, has his wife on the books, and that just doesn't work in the public arena.'[15]

schizophrenia, with responsibilities to the current shareholders as well as an interest in the new shareholders.

An MBO will depend for its success on the quality of the management team, and on the business's ability to raise money for the deal. Many MBOs involve the new management team finding significant sources of finance, and unsurprisingly many MBO-type deals are highly 'leveraged'. In other words there's a lot of debt involved. MBOs are often financed by venture capitalists – in which case the deal will share the characteristics of all venture capital backed deals: a good growth opportunity to enable the venture capitalist to look forward to excellent returns; a fit with the venture capitalist's own strategy and expertise; and a certain critical mass. Venture capitalists will want the deal to be of a certain size, to justify the costs of researching and executing the deal. The venture capitalist will also want to see a way out. He will want his money back and his return, and will want to be able to see how this will be achieved from the begin-

Outline of MBO process

ning. The venture capitalist will also want the management team to suffer a bit – to ensure that they are properly focused on realising the growth that will earn the return the venture capitalist is looking for. Management team members will be required to invest their own money as part of the deal. And though personal guarantees are unlikely to be required nowadays, the financiers will almost certainly want to take the management's shares in the new business as security. The management team's equity stake is often known as 'sweat equity', and for good reasons. The sweat will come from the hard work. The venture capitalist will not be too concerned if the sweat is also a consequence of nervous tension and worry.

There is no such thing as the typical MBO – all are different, but some of the variants have become sufficiently common to earn themselves acronyms of their own. A good opportunity may risk being spoiled by the quality of the management team; in which case the old management team may

> **'Having bought your way** into a leveraged MBO structure you have probably achieved the easy bit. All you now need to do is deliver the business plan and secure a profitable exit.' Derek Lovelock and Richard Glanville of Oasis Stores Plc

be replaced by a new one placed with the blessing of the financiers – a 'management buy-in', or MBI. And an MBO with a couple of experienced new managers joining the team to add significant missing skills is often referred to as a 'BIMBO'.

Often the sale of a business or part thereof involves a deal that is too small for a venture capitalist – and the minimum amount venture capitalists are prepared to invest in seems to get bigger and bigger. A 'business angel' – a private investor looking for investment opportunities – may be prepared to help fund a smaller deal or younger business.

A transaction of this sort – whether trade sale, MBO or some other form of transfer – is complicated and expensive, and you'll need to get good professional help, and be prepared to pay for it. There's much more to do than get an accountant's report signed off. Negotiating the deal, securing the finance, deal execution and project management all demand a reliable corporate finance adviser. There will be many complex tax issues to consider. There is a complicated legal framework – particularly if one of the parties is a public

---

Grooming the business for sale – some key questions

- ▨ Do you have an effective strategy for future growth? Can you communicate it? Do your financial projections support the strategy and make sense?
- ▨ Are your financial controls robust?
- ▨ What investment do you need to make in your business to ready it for sale, and what investments can be postponed for the new owners to make?
- ▨ Do you have a quality *second*-tier management team to look after the ship once you've gone?
- ▨ Are management incentivised and motivated to help with the sale process?
- ▨ Is there any outstanding or threatened litigation?
- ▨ Have you properly registered your intellectual property – patents, trademarks, domain names?
- ▨ Is it the right time yet to sell your business?
- ▨ After you've answered all the above, have you taken good-quality tax advice?

---

company. And if you're buying, then there is due diligence that will need to be performed to evaluate the deal opportunity – and you will not want the accountant who is doing your due diligence also to be acting as your lead corporate finance adviser, because that would lead to an obvious conflict of interest. And don't forget that due diligence doesn't just cover finance – there are the people, the environment, and the commercial future of the business to consider. It's unsurprising that a deal costs a lot of money and takes a lot of time.

But once the business is sold, it's time for the owner to start all over again. For the owner who's sold as well as for the

owner who's just bought, the sale of the business is a new
beginning.

- Most owners should give more attention to selling their
  own business and less to buying other people's
- An IPO is difficult, very expensive, and changes the
  business dramatically
- Whichever route to exit you take, good advice is critical,
  from someone who's been there before – and many times
- You may not know you're for sale. An offer out of the blue
  will flatter you at first – but ultimately may cause
  enormous disruption
- An earn-out may look like a good idea on paper – but can
  cause big problems after the transaction if not properly put
  together
- An MBO, if well planned and well put together, is one of
  the safest routes to an exit for the owner-manager

6

Useful information

Types of staff share plan

Approved Share Plan – a scheme that is approved by the Inland Revenue and gives its members and their employers certain tax advantages – in return for stringent conditions, of course.

Employee Share Ownership Trust (ESOT) – a trust established for the purpose of holding shares. Employees buy shares from and sell them to the trust, thus creating some sort of internal 'market' for otherwise untradeable securities.

Enterprise Management Incentive (EMI) – one of the current 'approved' schemes, and usually thought of as the most flexible. Designed to incentivise those involved in high-growth, entrepreneurial businesses, allowing them income and capital gains tax benefits on options over company shares in certain types of business.

Free Share Schemes. An 'unapproved scheme' in which the shares are given to employees either free of any restrictions, or with restrictions that prevent them from being sold for a period of time.

Phantom Share Option – not a share option at all, but a bonus that is designed to behave as if it were a share option.

Restricted Share Schemes subject to risk of forfeiture. These 'unapproved' schemes provide shares to the employee on terms that the shares may be forfeit at some time in the future. The employee is entitled to the shares when they are issued and may also be entitled to dividends and voting rights, although the shares themselves will normally be held in a trust on terms that prevent the employee from selling them while they can still be forfeit.

Long Term Incentive Plans. 'Unapproved' schemes in which the employee is promised or allocated a certain number of shares, but does not become entitled to the shares until the conditions set out are satisfied.

Share Option – a right to buy a share at a future date at a predetermined price. Option schemes may be 'approved' or 'unapproved' – and thus have varying degrees of tax efficiency.

Share Purchase Schemes. The shares are purchased by employees at a discount from the market value. The shares are either free of any restrictions, or carry restrictions that prevent them from being sold for a period of time.

Unapproved Share Plan – not one that is illegal, or even one that is waiting approval, but one that does not fall into the category of schemes 'approved' by the Inland Revenue that benefit from a tax incentive.

Other reading

For a full copy of the DIAMOND model, write to BDO Stoy Hayward, 8 Baker Street, London, W1U 3LL.

The New Business Road Test – What entrepreneurs and executives should do before writing a business plan, John Mullins, FT Prentice Hall, 2003. As good as anything on what to do before you've put your business together.

The Origin and Evolution of New Businesses, Amar Bhide, OUP, 2000. Still the best thing written on entrepreneurs and the businesses they found.

Infectious Greed, Frank Partnoy, Profile Books, 2003. Highly recommended if you are interested in a terrifying exposé of the new world of financial instruments and derivatives in big business.

The Company, John Micklethwait and Adrian Wooldridge, Weidenfeld & Nicolson, 2003. An excellent, concise history of the limited company, which is also, in passing, a history of management and organisation theory.

www.british-franchise.org The website of the British Franchise Association, a useful source of information on how to go about putting together a franchise.

www.franchisebusiness.co.uk Another useful source of information on franchising.

A Behavioural Finance Perspective on IPOs and SEOs, Burton, Helliar and Power, ACCA, Research Report 82, 2003. This doesn't sound like a riveting read. But it contains the qualitative and quantitative results of an interesting survey on those who have recently raised money on the stock markets, including through an IPO. It's also available on line from the ACCA's website, www.acca.co.uk

Alliance Advantage, the art of creating value through partnering, Gary Hamel and Yves Doz, Harvard Business School Press, 1998. One of the most interesting books on joint venture strategies and objectives and the benefits to be derived from them.

7

Acknowledgements

MANY THANKS AS always to those of my colleagues who have helped at various stages of this project – Peter Leach, Philip Rubenstein, Simon Bevan, Richard Childs, Jeremy Newman and Matthew Champkin.

Particular thanks are owed to Andrew Ware and David Ellis who reviewed and commented on Chapters 4 and 5. Charles Boundy has also, once again, reviewed the whole text. Any remaining technical errors are of course my own.

Thanks also to Andrew Franklin and Paul Forty at Profile.

Although it was a long time ago, and they're no longer around to consult, Richard Emanuel and Clint Evans were hugely influential on the thinking behind the DIAMOND growth model, along with Philip Rubinstein and Jo Watson.

8

Notes

1 As reported in the *Independent*, 30 January 2004
2 Andrew Carnegie, quoted in *The Company*, John
  Micklethwait and Adrian Wooldridge (Weidenfeld &
  Nicolson, 2003)
3 Section 459, Companies Act, 1985
4 'Evolution and revolution as organisations grow', Larry
  Greiner, *Harvard Business Review*, July/August 1972
5 Quoted in *The Origin and Evolution of New Business*,
  Amar Bhide (OUP, 2000)
6 'The five stages of business growth', Neil Churchill and
  Virginia Lewis, *Harvard Business Review*, June 1983 –
  and reprinted in *Harvard Business Review* since, and in a
  revised form in *Mastering Enteprise*, ed. Sue Birley and
  Daniel Muzyka (Pitman, 1997)
7 'Critical stages of small business growth', Lawrence
  Steinmetz, *Business Horizons*, February 1969
8 Retold in *The Company*, John Micklethwait and Adrian
  Wooldridge (Weidenfeld & Nicolson, 2003). The
  authors go on to point out that Ford's approach was
  disastrous for the Ford Motor Co., in its battle for
  market share with General Motors.

9 'Taking stock', Roger Martin, *Harvard Business Review*, January 2003

10 John England, Towers Perrin, quoted in 'What's wrong with executive compensation?', *Harvard Business Review*, January 2003

11 'For the last time: stock options are an expense', Zvi Bodie, Robert Kaplan, Robert Merton, *Harvard Business Review*, March 2003

12 'A behavioural finance perspective on IPOs and SEOs', B. Burton, C. Helliar and D. Power, *ACCA Research Report 82*, 2003

13 Ibid.

14 Quoted in 'A behavioural finance perspective on IPOs and SEOs', B. Burton, C. Helliar and D. Power, *ACCA Research Report 82*, 2003

15 Ibid.

Non-executive Directors
A BDO Stoy Hayward Guide for Growing Businesses
by Rupert Merson

The role of the non-executive director has never before come under such scrutiny. From once being seen as 'about as useful as Christmas tree decorations', non-executives are now seen as critical components in the corporate governance framework, and important contributors to the strategic health of companies.

Rupert Merson explores the particular contribution the non-executive can make in the younger, growing, owner-managed business.

ISBN 1 86197 499 X

£6.99

Managing Directors
A BDO Stoy Hayward Guide for Growing Businesses
by Rupert Merson

The problems of running a growing business are very different from those of running a big business. Growing businesses have their own specific needs, which are not widely understood.

Rupert Merson's helpful and entertaining guide is essential reading for all those who run, hope to run or are looking for someone to run a business of this kind. It focuses on the key aspects of the managing director's role, and how to relate to the ambitions of the business's owner.

ISBN 1 86197 740 9

£6.99

An Inspector Returns
The A–Z to surviving a tax investigation
by Daniel Dover & Tim Hindle
with cartoons by Michael Heath

Revised and updated second edition

If you are the subject of a tax investigation by the Inland Revenue, do not panic – read this book instead. An investigation undoubtedly means trouble, but the straightforward advice in these pages should help steer you around the worst pitfalls and survive the process intact.

'An amusing guide through this difficult subject … This disarmingly honest little book could save you many sleepless nights.' *The Times*

ISBN 1 86197 420 5

£6.99

War or Peace
Skirmishes with the Revenue
by Daniel Dover & Tim Hindle
with cartoons by McLachlan

Each year over 250,000 people are subject to Inland Revenue enquiries. It is not a pleasant experience. But help is at hand. For the first time here is a book that explains the whole process, along with numerous tips on how to proceed and what to do – or not to do. Deftly written with wit and humour, this could save you time, misery and money.

ISBN 1 86197 524 4

£6.99